Flip the Flaps
Jungle Animals

Jinny Johnson and Nicki Palin

KINGFISHER

KINGFISHER

First published 2009 by Kingfisher
This edition published 2012 by Kingfisher
an imprint of Macmillan Children's Books
a division of Macmillan Publishers Limited
20 New Wharf Road, London N1 9RR
Basingstoke and Oxford
Associated companies throughout the world
www.panmacmillan.com

Consultant: David Burnie

ISBN 978-0-7534-3461-1

1 3 5 7 9 8 6 4 2
1TR/0911/UNTD/LFA/157MA

A CIP catalogue record for this book is available from the British Library.

Printed in China

Contents

Life in the jungle

Jungles are big forests that grow in places where it is very hot all the time. It rains nearly every day, too, so jungles are always wet. In fact, another name for jungle is rainforest.

There are thousands of plants in a rainforest.

parrots

sloth

golden lion tamarin

giant anteater

4

howler
monkey

spider
monkey

1. Do lots of animals
live in the jungle?

2. Do some of them live
up in the trees?

emerald
boa snake

3. What happens at
night in the jungle?

1. Yes. More kinds of animal live in jungles than anywhere else on earth.

harpy eagle

The jungle at night

The comet moth flies at night.

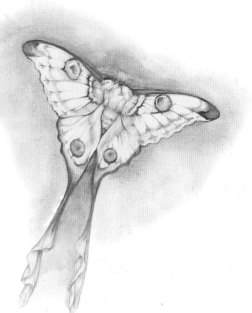

2. Yes. Many jungle animals live in the trees. Some of them never come down!

The tarsier has big eyes for seeing in the dark.

3. It's very dark, but busy! Lots of jungle creatures sleep during the day and wake up at night.

The fishing bat snatches fish from the water.

Brilliant birds

Some of the world's most amazing and colourful birds live in jungles. But it can be hard to spot them in the tangled trees. Parrots, toucans, hummingbirds and birds of paradise all live in the jungle.

male bird of paradise

female bird of paradise

6

1. Which are the most beautiful jungle birds?

2. Why do birds of paradise have colourful feathers?

3. What do jungle birds eat?

hanging
upside down

1. Male birds of paradise have some of the most spectacular feathers of all.

2. Males show off their colourful feathers to attract females. This one hangs upside down and rocks to and fro.

3. Many jungle birds eat plant foods. Their beaks are specially shaped to help them gather their food.

Beak shapes

hummingbird

sucking nectar with its long, thin beak

toucan

picking berries with its long beak

parrot

cracking a nut with its strong beak

Apes and monkeys

Apes and many kinds of monkeys live in jungles. Gorillas, chimpanzees and orang-utans are all apes. Fruit and leaves are their favourite foods. Apes are our closest relatives in the animal kingdom.

durian fruit

mother and baby orang-utan

3

1. What is the difference between apes and monkeys?

2. How does an orang-utan move around the jungle?

3. What do apes and monkeys do all day?

swinging
from a vine

1. Apes do not have tails, but most monkeys have long tails.

2. She swings from tree to tree on her long arms. Her arms are nearly twice as long as her body!

3. Looking for food takes up most of the day, but they also play, groom each other and rest.

During the day...

Chimpanzee

using a stick to collect insects to eat

Gorillas

taking a midday nap

Squirrel monkey

grooming her baby

River life

A huge river flows through this jungle. It may look calm, but it is full of life, with huge snakes, crocodiles and lots of fish. People can use rivers to travel through the jungle, too.

insect on a branch

archerfish

capybaras

anaconda snake

caiman hiding underwater

10

1. How does an archerfish catch its food?

2. Which are the most fierce animals in the river?

3. What other creatures live in jungle rivers?

jet of water

caiman attacks

1. The archerfish spits at an insect and knocks it down into the water. Then the fish gobbles up the insect.

2. Caimans are fierce animals. They lie with only their eyes and nose above the water, then make a surprise attack.

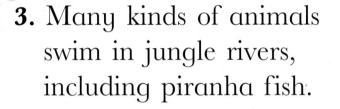

3. Many kinds of animals swim in jungle rivers, including piranha fish.

Other animals in the river

Piranha fish have sharp teeth.

The matamata turtle looks like a clump of bark and leaves.

River dolphins eat fish, crabs and turtles.

Jungle hunters

Many jungle creatures feed
on leaves, flowers and fruit.
But there are plenty
of meat-eaters around,
too. They hunt the
plant-eating animals.

tiger

jaguar mum
and cubs

12

1. Why do jungle cats
have spots and stripes?

2. Which are the biggest
hunters in the jungle?

3. What other hunters are
there in the jungle?

tiger hiding in grass

jaguar roaring to scare
other animals away

1. Spots and stripes help big cats hide among jungle plants as they creep up on their prey.

2. The tiger is the biggest jungle hunter of all. But jaguars are nearly as large.

3. Birds hunt in the treetops, while ocelots hunt lower down. Bush dogs catch food on the forest floor.

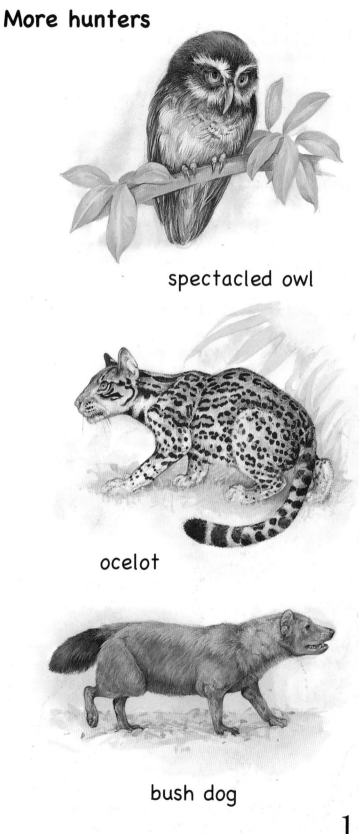

spectacled owl

ocelot

bush dog

Insects and spiders

There are more insects than any other type of animal in the jungle, and lots of spiders, too. Ants, beetles, butterflies and many others live on every tree, as well as on the forest floor.

leaf-cutter ant

The forest floor is full of life.

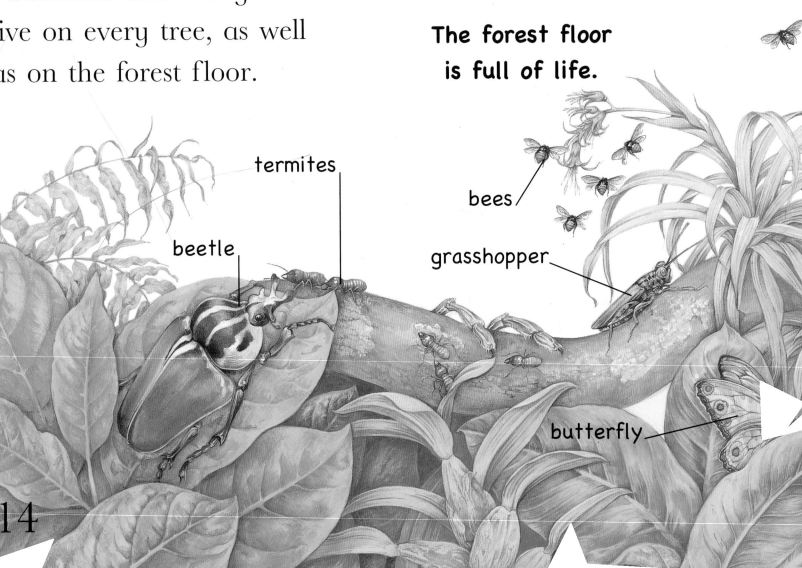

termites

beetle

bees

grasshopper

butterfly

14

1. What do leaf-cutter ants do with the leaves they collect?

2. Are there big spiders in the jungle?

3. How do insects hide from their enemies?

_____ katydid

ants carrying leaves

butterfly
flying away

goliath
bird-eating
spider

1. They take them to their nest and chew them up. Then they grow fungi (tiny mushrooms) on the leaves for food.

grasshopper hopping away

2. Yes. The largest spider in the world, the goliath bird-eating spider, is as big as a dinner plate!

3. Often they are disguised to look like something else, such as a flower.

katydid

Can you find the flower mantis?

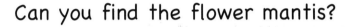

Can you see the stick insect?

15

Frogs, snakes and lizards

These creatures like to live in warm, damp places, so jungles are just right. Many spend time up in the trees as well as on the ground. Snakes are good climbers – even though they have no legs.

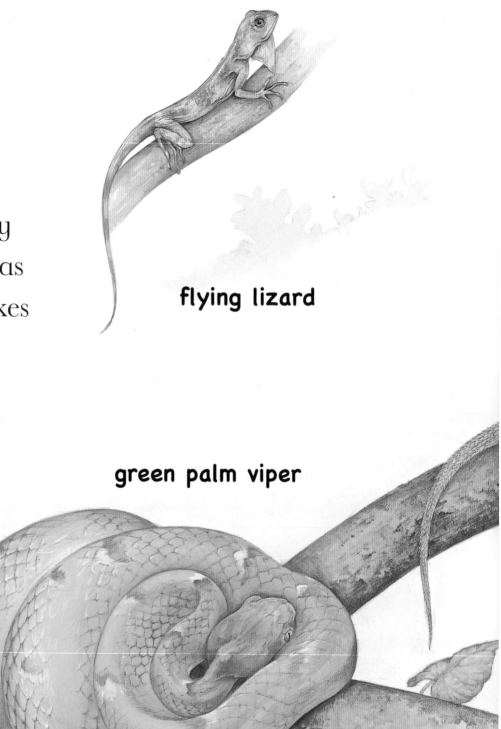

flying lizard

green palm viper

1. Does a flying lizard
really fly?

2. What do snakes eat?

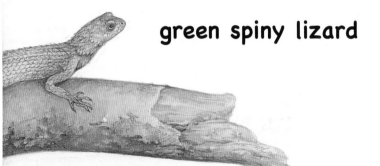

green spiny lizard

3. Why are some frogs
so brightly coloured?

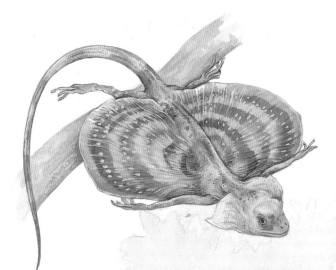

gliding through the air

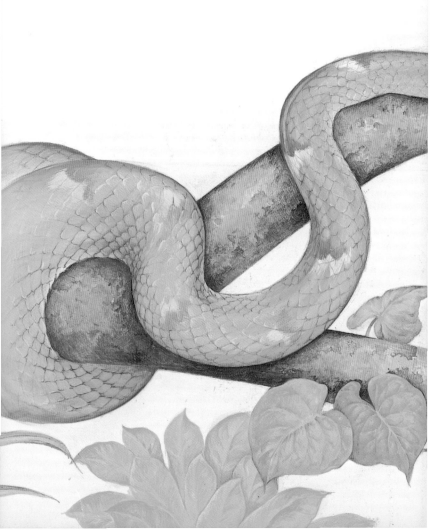

1. It doesn't really fly, but can glide through the air from tree to tree. It uses flaps on its body like a parachute.

2. Snakes are meat-eaters. They catch other animals and swallow them whole.

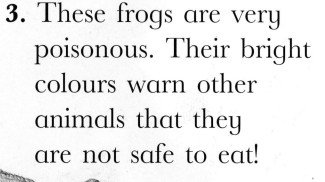

3. These frogs are very poisonous. Their bright colours warn other animals that they are not safe to eat!

Tree frogs can be...

green and black

strawberry-red

blue

or yellow and black

17

Index